# LOG CABINS

## HOW TO BUILD AND FURNISH THEM

# Log Cabins

## HOW TO BUILD AND FURNISH THEM

WILLIAM S. WICKS

Skyhorse Publishing

Skyhorse Publishing books may be purchased in bulk at special discounts for sales promotion, corporate gifts, fund-raising, or educational purposes. Special editions can also be created to specifications. For details, contact the Special Sales Department, Skyhorse Publishing, 307 West 36th Street, 11th Floor, New York, NY 10018 or info@skyhorsepublishing.com.

Skyhorse® and Skyhorse Publishing® are registered trademarks of Skyhorse Publishing, Inc.®, a Delaware corporation.

Visit our website at www.skyhorsepublishing.com.

10 9 8 7 6 5 4 3 2 1

Library of Congress Cataloging-in-Publication Data

Wicks, William S.
  Log cabins : how to build and furnish them / by William S. Wicks.
     p. cm.
  ISBN 978-1-61608-184-3 (pb : alk. paper)
  1. Log cabins--Design and construction. I. Title.
  TH4840.W535 2011
  690'.837--dc22
       2010036072

Print ISBN: 978-1-63220-706-7
Ebook ISBN: 978-1-62636-660-2

Printed in the United States of America

# CONTENTS

# LOG CABINS

OME recent anthropologists regard the amusements of the chase, as cultivated by civilized men—hunting, fishing, and the like—as "traces in modern civilization of original barbarism." If there is any truth in this theory, then the writer must confess that he is in a large measure a barbarian. But for years of devotion to life in the woods—a devotion that is paralleled only in the religious devotee—this little book would not have been written. Because the writer loves camp-life, and wishes to augment its pleasures, he sends forth this little volume, sure that his effort will be appreciated by all those in whom can be found "traces of original barbarism." The theme, Log Cabins, How to Build and Furnish Them, may savor a little too much of the technical and practical. But, then, as the most beautiful and fragrant flowers and delicious fruits must have their roots in the soil, so all the higher and more ethereal

pleasures and benefits must, in civilization, be rooted in the practical and technical.

If in the desire for a return to the woods you discover elements of an uncivilized condition, that is no reason why you should go to the woods in a barbaric fashion. The modern representative of city life must not dream of going to the woods and living like a savage "in caves and dens of the earth," nor must he attempt to assume the remoter "arboreal habits" of the "hairy biped." As man has brought with him from barbarism to civilization traces of his original condition, so he must take back to "the forest primeval" some traces of his civilization. There is one obvious difference between our remote ancestors and ourselves. They lived in caves and dens, hunted and fished, because of necessity and inability to live in any other way. We migrate to the woods, hunt and fish from choice; we go for change, recuperation, pleasure, health. We aim to treasure up energies in order to better sustain the tension of civilization. Health is imperative, and demands a dwelling in the woods in many points resembling a civilized one.

Camp structures may be classified as temporary and permanent. The temporary include the various forms of "shelter" illustrated and described on pages 87 to 100; the permanent, that class of buildings made with more durable materials than the "shelter"—such as stones, logs, slabs, shingle or bark. The temporary class of structures is referred to only because in almost every case a shelter must precede the permanent structure.

The choice of material for a camp is, to a large extent, a matter of taste, expense or convenience. In the judgment of the writer no material equals the log, and no cabin looks so well as the log cabin. One essential of both a log cabin and its furniture is, that as far as possible both must be made on the spot and with the material at hand.

# 1

# LOCATION OF
# CAMP

The location of the camp will be determined by considerations of health, taste, pleasure, and convenience. Health is paramount. Be sure that your cabin is on elevated ground, away from swales, swamp and boggy lands. Good water is indispensable. Get as near as possible to a small, swift running brook. Failing in this, be sure that you have a spring, or can secure good water by digging a "pocket" or hole in the ground for a reservoir.

In a lake site a little sheltering bay is desirable; it will give protection to both cabin and boat house. The water should be deep enough for a good boat landing, and at the same time have a shelving and sandy beach for an occasional bath. It is full as well, however, to have the sand beach a short distance from the camp, to give a chance for a little exercise before and after the bath.

In selecting a site, beautiful scenery must not be ignored. Those who regard the sporting instincts in man as relics of barbarism inform us that the love of scenery is one of the distinguishing characteristics of the civilized man, and that it is only within the last two hundred years that man has learned to love rocks, hills, woods, mountains, lakes, seas and clouds for their own intrinsic loveliness; and that even now the taste for scenery on a large scale is confined to comparatively few races, and comparatively few persons among them. Love lovely scenery, and in selecting your camp site pick out a commanding position. You should be able to see long distances over water as well as over a succession of hills and mountains. Certainly, the camping regions abound in so much beautiful scenery that it would be a shame if any but the most delightful points were selected.

However healthful and beautiful the camp site may be, if its approaches from the outer world are laboriously difficult and attended with too many practical discomforts, it will be found exceedingly difficult to appreciate the scenery. Camp approaches should be as accessible as possible from all places of interest and pleasure resorts. Quick time and easy transit are as important in the woods as in the city.

Be sure that in the near vicinity of your camp you have straight timber suitable for building purposes. Should your location be on a lake shore or river bank, however, it may be possible for you to float your logs from a distance. These and similar considerations must guide you in locating your camp.

Having selected your site, the next thing is to study it. Mark well its commanding and beautiful views, its background, the foreground. Study it as you would a painting, for out of your site and its environment must grow your building plan. Indeed, the structure should be the outgrowth of, and harmonize with the site, so that when your cabin is completed it shall be a new object added by the hand of man to perfect and beautify its surroundings; and the whole when viewed shall produce an agreeable effect, like harmony in music and rhythm in poetry. Hence the difficulties attending the choice of a building plan. As every man needs to be measured to get a perfectly fitting garment, so every building site needs to be considered to get a perfectly suitable cabin. The sketches found in this volume are susceptible to many changes and combinations with others. Some of them may, like a ready-made coat, fit you fairly well; still, they are only intended to assist in formulating your ideas.

To obtain the best result it might be well to secure the aid of a professional architect, one skilled in woodcraft. Give him the best description you can of the site and its environment. Better, of course, if you take the architect with you to see and measure your site. Give him a liberal commission to make drawings;

the percentage should be a great deal larger than the usual fee. Tell him all your little desires and whims and what you wish to accomplish and at what cost; or, if the cost does not enter into the question, so much the better.

# 2

# STAKING OUT AND PREPARING FOR WORK

Having your plans, now stake out the size of your building, so that you may know the distance to level off the ground round about. Cut down trees that may be in the way of the cabin and no more, unless there are rotten and unsound trees standing near. These fell at once, or a wind-storm may throw one or more across your cabin.

If possible your living-room should face the east, south-east, or south. If it is your intention to build an ice-house, or store-house, build it at once, as it will serve the purpose of a shelter while the principal work is progressing. For temporary convenience, however, it may be better to build a simple lean-to (see Fig. 47) of the tops and branches of the trees felled to make room for the cabin.

# 3

# FOUNDATIONS

Do not be careless about the foundations; secure the best material that the vicinity of your camp will afford. If you use posts, select sound timber from ten to twelve inches in diameter, either hemlock, pine, tamarack, or cedar. Cedar is the best. The hard woods will do, but they are not as durable.

The posts should be cut about five feet long, though a little less will do. Holes must be dug in the ground large enough to receive the posts, and at least three feet deep, or deep enough for the bottom end of the posts to rest on solid ground or rock. Place one post under each angle or corner, and as many more under the sides as are needed. For instance, if the cabin is rectangular, say twenty feet by twelve feet, then under the twenty feet side there should be two posts between the corners and under the twelve feet side one post. After the posts are in position mark one, say ten inches from the highest ground, and cut it off square; then from this mark its level on all the others and cut them off square, in order to begin your first tier of logs on a perfectly level foundation.

Cutting the posts at the same height applies when the logs are laid according to the second method, shown in Fig. 3, but not when the logs are laid according to the first method, or lock-joint, as shown in Fig. 2. If the lock-joint method is adopted, the posts at the ends of the building, not including the corner ones, should be cut off some four inches higher than the others, or half the thickness of the logs that you are using, owing to the unequal height of the end and side logs. The posts are left ten inches above ground to secure a good circulation of air beneath the floor timbers.

If stone is to be used for foundation piers, dig holes three feet or more in depth and not less than two feet in diameter. Fill these holes with small or broken stones up to the level of the ground, taking care that the stones are well settled together. Now get large cobble-stones and place them directly on top of the broken stone, chinking them up with small stone so that they will be well–bedded in place. As with the posts, be careful that the cobble or cap-stones are high enough above ground and level to receive the first tier of logs.

If the ground is firm it will do nearly as well to simply bed large stones in the ground and do away with the pits; in fact, this is the usual way. If a cellar is built under the cabin it will, of course, make the best foundation. The wall should be about eighteen inches thick and laid up of the best stone that can be procured in the vicinity. Use mortar as directed under the subject of chimneys.

# 4

# SELECTION OF
# TIMBER

The logs best suited for building must be straight, sound, and uniform in size; they may vary from six inches to ten inches in diameter. Spruce, pine, hemlock, tamarack, and balsam are the best. The hard woods will serve the purpose, but they are very heavy to handle, especially when green. The tops of the trees, if straight, will work in for joists and rafters. The first step is to make a careful bill of quantities, or list of all the logs you will need, giving the size and length of each, together with the place in which it is to be used.

As the outside of the cabin will look much better with the rough bark showing, the best time to cut the logs is when the bark will not peel during the drying. In the northern part of New York State all logs should be cut from October to February, not much before October nor later than February.

The time of year best suited to building log cabins varies largely according to the locality. It depends on the snow and rain-fall. In the Adirondack region the snow is very deep after December, while in the spring months the sap is in the tree and the bark will easily peel. This leaves only the fall months in which to build; probably in October and November is the best time. There is not then the difficulty of hauling logs to the camp through the deep snow, and the bark at this time clings tightly to the trees.

While hauling the logs to camp care must be taken to preserve the bark intact. If a chain is fastened around one end of the log and it is drawn on the ground for a short distance, on reaching camp the bark will be found to be bruised and torn. The best way to get the logs to camp is to secure one end to a log boat and thus haul to the skids.

All logs must be cut at least two feet longer than the given length or width of the building. If the building is to be twelve by fourteen feet, outside measurement, then the logs must be cut fourteen and sixteen feet long respectively. This does not apply when the logs are laid as shown in Fig. 3. There is in this case only one end of the log which extends outside of the cabin, and for this reason only one foot needs to be added to the outside size of the cabin to get the proper length of logs.

The logs having been cut, they should be hauled to camp, and in order to keep them out of dirt and mud, must be placed on logs, or skids, as they are

Fig. I

commonly called (Fig. 1). Each length and size should be placed by itself, ready to be examined and used. Select the strongest, largest and best-shaped for the sills or first tier of logs. These must have the upper side hewn or flattened to a straight line from end to end, so that the space in the narrowest part of the log is about three or four inches in width. Use the utmost care in fitting these sills to the rocks or posts, so that the flattened surfaces or upper sides will be level with each other and entirely out of wind. The rest of the logs used for sides of the cabin, or minor partitions, must be flattened both top and bottom; take one at a time to the building and place it on the logs already in position. The lock joint or log house corner is made with the axe, so when the logs are placed in position the flat surfaces will come close together. In making this joint the log on the underside is to be cut in a V shape, and the one placed on top in a reverse V shape (Fig. 2), and while being fitted the upper may need to be rolled in and out of place a number of times before a perfect joint is obtained.

In constructing the frame work of a cabin with the lock joint, the side and end logs of each tier do not come at even height; and to obviate this difficulty some woodsmen frame the timber as shown in the sketch below (Fig. 3). When the logs are laid in this way, each tier should be pinned to the one directly underneath. To do this, bore an inch and a quarter auger hole through the top stick and half way through the under one, and drive a hardwood pin into the hole to secure the logs firmly in position.

As soon as the first tier of logs is laid, cut out the notches, or gains, and lay the sleepers (Fig. 5). These will be spoken of later under the head of "Joists."

Now continue laying up each tier of logs, alternating the butts and tops, so that the wall will present a uniform appearance. Make no particular calculations for the openings, unless it be to place a poor part of the stick where it will eventually be cut away. When you have reached the height of the windows and doors, saw out the top logs of these spaces and lay the following

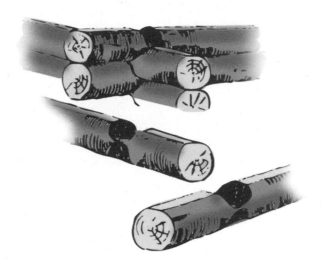

Fig. 2

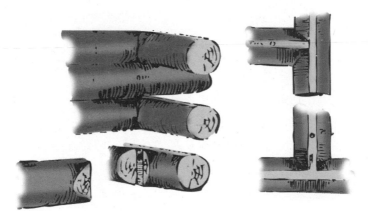

Fig. 3

tier. Then finish the openings by cutting the logs below the one already sawed out. This may be accomplished in the most satisfactory way by two men using a cross-cut saw. The openings being made, they will give you much more freedom to work in and about the building. The door and window frames should be ready to put in place, so as to nail them fast, and thus secure the loose ends of the logs coming to these openings (Fig. 4).

When at the height of the second floor, frame and place this tier of joist and again continue with the laying up of logs to the proper height for receiving the rafters, proceeding in the same way for the second story openings as described above.

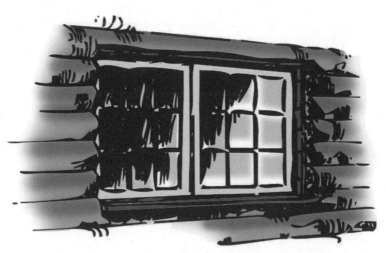

Fig. 4

# 5

# JOISTS

The sleepers, or joists, as they are more frequently called, are to be gained and tenoned into the bearing timbers (Fig. 5), and so placed that they will have the shortest possible span. Those supporting the first floor may be left rough, as they do not show, but those in the second story and ceiling will look best if they are peeled of their bark. Often these joists are made of hewn square timbers and with excellent effect, as shown in the sketch (Fig. 6).

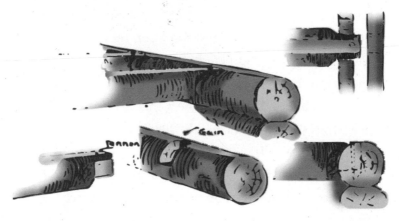

Fig. 5

Fig. 6

Select for the joist straight, sound trees. The logs for a twelve feet span or less should be about six inches in diameter; for a sixteen feet span eight inches in diameter; for a twenty feet span nine or ten inches in diameter. They should have one face flattened from end to end to make an even surface for the floors to rest on. This face in a twenty feet joist should crown in the centre about two inches; for when they are put in place they will sag sufficiently with their own weight and that of the floors, to make them level.

Joists, and indeed all timbers that are flattened or hewn into shape, are formed by hewing to a chalk-line with a broad-axe. It is astonishing to see the amount of work that a skillful carpenter can accomplish in a day with these tools. Place the joist from two to three feet apart, according to size and strength, also calculating somewhat on the quality of the flooring. The joist should be framed and placed as the building progresses. The gains are framed in the logs, and the tenons are made on the joist, as indicated in the fore-going sketch. They are then placed and pinned or spiked to hold them fast and keep the building from spreading.

Place a good stiff timber directly under every partition running the same way as the joist, even though it may makc irregular spacing of the joist in

Fig. 7

Fig. 8

21

the ceiling below. For openings in the floor, such as are needed for stairs, chimneys, trap-doors, hearths, etc., if the space between the joist is not large enough, a joist must be cut; and in this case a cross-piece, or header, must be secured by gain and tenon or spikes to the joist on either side; the end of the cut joist must be framed and secured to the header (Fig. 7).

Always leave a little space between wood-work and chimneys or smoke-pipes, on account of fire. Never at any time must the ends of timbers rest on the chimneys, unless the brick and stone are built out in a little ledge or corbel, to receive them (Fig. 8). If the wood extends too near the flues it is liable to get charred and thus catch fire.

# 6

# THE ROOF

The pitch of a roof is the proportion existing between its width and rise of angle; thus a third-pitch roof is one which has one foot of rise in every three feet of width. The pitch should in the main be governed by the nature of the covering, though partially by the taste of the designer. The high-pitch roof presents the best qualities; it shoots off the snow and rain; the wind will not blow the water and fine snow under the shingles; nor can it so easily strip the roof of its covering. The steep roof is, however, more expensive to build,

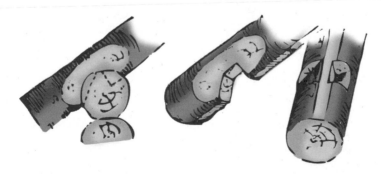

Fig. 9

because there is more covering, and the timbers need to be longer and larger.

The rafters should be selected and flattened in the same manner as the joist were. Frame them on to the plate-logs at the bottom (Fig. 9), and bevel them at the top end to suit the pitch of the roof.

Place a ridge-board or pole between the rafters at the top end. Raise the gable and hip-rafters first, as they will serve as guides in placing the rest. After these are in position it may be found necessary to cut off or block up the intervening ones a little to fit the ridge-pole or board, and thus make a perfectly straight roof line. Place the rafters from two to three feet apart. Pin or spike them at the foot to the log-plates, and at the top nail them to the ridge-pole.

For an ordinary shingle roof the boards may be one inch by four inch strips, placed two inches apart, or thereabouts, to suit the weathering of the shingle. If it is difficult to get the boards four or five inches in diameter, small timber will answer very well. Flatten them on one side and halve them on to the rafters. Do not cut the rafters any more than necessary to make a good bearing because it will weaken them too much to bear the heavy winter snows. Nail these pieces to place, the same as if they were boards. Let the sticks or boards, whichever you use, project over the gable ends

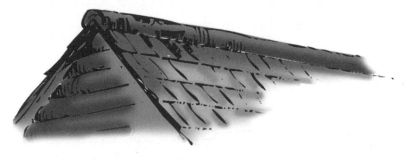

Fig. 10

as far as you want the roof to extend, but not less than six inches, so that you may be sure of having the drip of the water fall away from the building.

The roof may be covered with different material, depending largely on the locality, the skill of the workmen, and the ease with which the material may be obtained. The shingle roof may have a pitch varying from one-quarter to one-half; sometimes even more than one-half; but never less than one-quarter. A shingle is technically four inches wide, but they vary largely as actually made. They are usually sold by the thousand, and two half-thousand bunches, or four quarter-thousand bunches, and must contain that number, four inches wide, or the equivalent. Shingles vary largely in their length, but should be at least sixteen inches long to make a good roof. For the lowest pitch-roof, lay four and one-quarter inches to the weather; other pitches may run as high as five inches to the weather.

The soft woods, spruce, pine, and hemlock, make the best shingles. They are made on the ground by the shingle-maker who splits them out of blocks of wood and shaves them into shape. One thousand shingles, if laid five inches to the weather, with no wasters, will cover one hundred and thirty square feet of surface. The first, or eave course of shingles, is usually laid double, so as not to be broken off by the snow or ice; and at the peak there should be a ridge-board placed to cover the top ends of the last course of shingles. This may be a ridge-pole made from a small log about four inches in diameter, cut out V shape (Fig. 10). A well-made shingle roof has an average life of about fifteen years.

# SHINGLES FOR SIDES OF CABIN

The second story gables, or indeed the entire sides of the cabin, may be enclosed with matched or ordinary boards nailed to upright pieces. These pieces should be placed about sixteen inches apart, and are held in position by a plate or horizontal piece nailed to the top ends. The boards, in turn, are covered with shingles the same as the roof. A lining of building paper will help to keep the cabin warm. A good effect may be made in this finish of shingle work by making the corner posts of rough timbers or logs, setting the upright pieces or studding flush with them on the inside. This will simply make a log corner. The second story may be made of slabs or half logs, as directed under head of partitions, but the ordinary log way is the most satisfactory of all, and it looks well to see the logs extending up the gables to the peak.

# BARK COVERINGS

Bark may be easily peeled only when the sap is well up the tree, but a skillful person will manage to procure it at almost any season of the year except mid-winter, and even then by cutting on the sunny side of the tree. The woodman simply cuts or girdles two rings around the tree from four to six feet apart, with one vertical cut connecting them; starting from this cut, and prying away on either side, little by little the whole cylinder of bark may be removed. The bark is much the best when

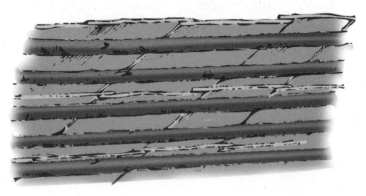

Fig. 11

taken from large trees, for, when flattened out, if from a small tree it is apt to split and break. After the bark is peeled it is laid on the ground to dry for some days, after which it can be flattened out by the weight of a few stones or logs placed on top. The bark may now be cut and used in the same general manner as shingles, or, as is more common, it may be laid in strips about four feet long and as wide as the circumference of the tree from which it is taken.

When a roof is laid of these long pieces, the bearing poles are laid horizontally and about two feet apart; the bark is then laid cross-wise with a lap of six inches (Fig. 11). This sort of a roof does very well for a temporary shelter, but will make neither a lasting roof nor a tight one.

# 9

# THATCH

The thatched roof must, of necessity, be steep; it should be built at an angle of forty-five degrees, or at one half pitch. If it is greater the straw will slide out, and if less the rain will not run off freely.

The rafters should be placed as for an ordinary roof, but if the lathing to which the thatching is bound is small and weak, they must be placed closer together. The lathing strips are made of strong round poles about one inch in diameter, placed horizontally at right angles to the rafters and about seven inches apart. Sawed strips of boards may be used instead of poles, though they would be weaker and would not last so long.

Before putting on a straw thatch the material should be thoroughly soaked with water and straightened so that the straw will lie all one way. Begin forming the eaves by binding on the first course to the roof sticks in bundles about four inches thick and twelve inches wide, with hemp, or, better still, tarred cording. This cord is passed by means of a large needle through the straw

Fig. 12

at the upper end of the bundles and tied around the laths, where it will be covered by the following course, each strip advancing to the ridge is made to overlap the preceding one as in shingling, though the space of straw exposed at the butt is much greater. When the strips are placed from eaves to ridge, comb the straw out straight with a wooden rake and finish off the ridge by plaiting the straw together. Cut the eaves off square and straight, and treat the hips in a similar manner to the ridges. The eave board or pole should be strong enough to bear the weight of a ladder with a man at work upon it while laying the first course of thatching.

A thatched roof presents the best appearance of all (Fig. 12), but there are so many little knacks in its construction that it is difficult for an amateur to build one successfully; but when thoroughly and skillfully made, one will last for twelve years and frequently much longer.

# 10

# FLOORS

Now that the roof is on and the cabin generally closed in, comes the question of floors. Spruce or pine flooring one inch thick and six inches wide, matched and planed, is good enough. Eight or nine inch boards are often used, but when they are as wide as this the shrinkage is sufficient to open the joint and let the dust and dirt through to the story below.

Plane the floors on both sides to make a smooth ceiling; or lay the floors in two thicknesses, the first thickness with smooth side down and diagonally. When buying your flooring be sure and get the boards of the right length to work to advantage, also be sure that every piece is sound and perfect before leaving the mill, so that there is nothing to be wasted when it reaches camp.

# 11

# INSIDE PARTITIONS

These are made in a variety of ways and are placed after the flooring is laid. The simplest and perhaps the most satisfactory manner of making such a partition is with matched boarding (Fig. 13).

If a particularly smooth job is wanted, have the boarding planed on both sides before leaving the mill. A cleat about one inch square with the corner taken off should be nailed to the ceiling or to ceiling beams at the top, and to the flooring boards at the bottom,

Fig. 13

care being taken that they are in line. The matched boards are then cut the proper length and placed in position, driving the matchings as tightly together as possible, but without nailing, save an occasional tack nail, which should be taken out at completion. Place on the opposite side of the boarding the same sort of a cleat as mentioned above, and the partition is completed. When partitions are built in this way the cracks which occur from shrinkage of boards may be entirely corrected by driving the boards together and putting in an additional piece to fill out the space at the side of the room. If, however, the matched boarding is not over five inches wide, and fairly dry, it is safe enough to use but one cleat and toe-nail to the flooring from the opposite side of the partition, and so also at the top, unless it should be found convenient to nail to the side of a timber or joist.

# A SECOND WAY

Use unmatched, planed or not–planed boards, and nail a vertical piece or batten about two inches wide and one inch thick over the joint (Fig. 14). In this case the boards should be nailed firmly at top and bottom, or, if it should be desirable to build so that the joint shrinkage may be taken up, as in the first example, then nail one batten to the edge of each board only, and proceed as there directed.

Fig. 14

# 13

# A THIRD WAY

Use slabs (Fig. 15). These are usually wasted or sold for fuel by the mills. Place them vertically and alternately, as shown in the sketch, and nail firmly at top and bottom and to each other.

If it is impossible or difficult to get slabs, a substitute may be made by halving logs and using in the same way as the slabs. This will make a stronger and better looking partition. The only difficulty is the splitting of the log. This is done so seldom that the ordinary workman hardly knows how to proceed, and therefore thinks that the difficulty is insurmountable. Still, there is not so much hard labor connected with it as one would suppose. The log to be divided is placed on strong saw horses. These horses should be about three feet high, and at a distance apart to accommodate the length of the log, which should be wedged to keep it from rocking; the workman then strikes a chalk line from end to end, gets on top of the log and saws it in halves with a large frame, or muley saw, as shown in Fig. 16, or with a heavy-bladed single-handled saw.

Fig. 15

The muley saw should be about two inches wide and four feet long, fastened and stretched in a good stout frame. With a full set, sharp saw, a good sized log may be cut very quickly. Of course, the better the workman the less amount of dressing- up there will be

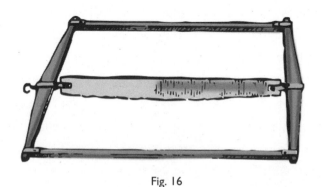

Fig. 16

afterwards. If, however, the saw should run a little, and the cut face be rough, a few strokes of the broad-axe, adz or jack-plane, will soon bring it into shape.

Logs cut in this way might be used for a variety of purposes, such as gable-ends, roofs, steps, shelves, or even for the outside partitions of the cabin. We would certainly advise any workman who is engaged in this sort of work to make the trial.

# 14

# A FOURTH WAY

Place straight sticks vertically about two feet apart; make one face of all the sticks as true to a line as possible; after securing these posts top and bottom place sheets of bark on them horizontally, each piece overlapping the preceding one a few inches (Fig. 17), in the same manner as bark is laid ft on a roof.

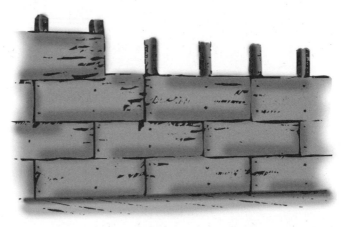

Fig. 17

# 15

# CHIMNEYS

If the cabin is to have the dignity of a chimney or fire-place, it should be built as the other work progresses. Make a good foundation of stone, beginning about three and a half feet below the surface, or on the rock. To make a stable piece of work, the foundation, as well as the entire chimney, should be laid up in cement mortar. The mortar may be made of any of the ordinary cements mixed with sand.

# 16

# FIRE-PLACES

The fire-place (Fig. 18) should be made of fire-brick and the rest of the chimney of ordinary brick; or if a stone chimney is preferred, have a lining of fire-brick for the fire-place.

The fire-place opening should seldom be over three feet high, and from three to five feet wide, and have a deep throat, so that the smoke will have a good easy start. The face of the fire-place can be built either of brick or stone, or both. The opening should be arched, or a stone lintel placed across to sustain the masonry above. Build ledges above the fire opening, on which to rest the mantel shelf. If the ledges are omitted, the mantel shelf can be supported with rustic brackets.

Be sure to have large smoke flues, at least twelve by twelve up to twenty by twenty inches in size, depending upon the dimensions of the fire-place. In the place of brick, sewer tile are frequently used for flues, but a small settlement will open the joints and thus give the fire a chance to reach and burn the timbers. To prevent the roof from leaking around the chimney, on the upper side, lay one edge of a piece of tin in the joints of the brick work, the other end under the shingles, raising the tin in the centre so that it will shoot the water away from the chimney. At thc bottom side lay a piece of tin in the joints of the brick-work, but over the shingles. On both ends of the chimney lay pieces of tin with each course of brick work. Let these pieces project two or three inches from the brick and turn down on the pieces of tin, which must be laid with each course of shingles. These tin shingles must be turned up on

Fig. 18

Fig. 19

one side high enough to come under (Fig. 19) the tin placed in the joints of the brick-work. The best draft is obtained by extending the chimney a foot or two above the ridge of the cabin. If, however, the roof is steep, and the chimney is placed at the eaves, its top may be made considerably lower than the ridge pole, but in this case it should be capped over on the top in an arch and opened at the edges, as shown above.

# 17

# SMOKE PIPE

If you intend to have a sheet-iron pipe for a smoke stack, let it go out through the roof so as not to make an extra elbow. At the shingle line place a tin or galvanized iron tube the same size as the smoke pipe and fitting into it at the first joint. Let this tube have a flange to fit the pitch of the roof. The upper edge of the flange must be pushed under a course of shingles and then nailed to the roof (Fig. 20).

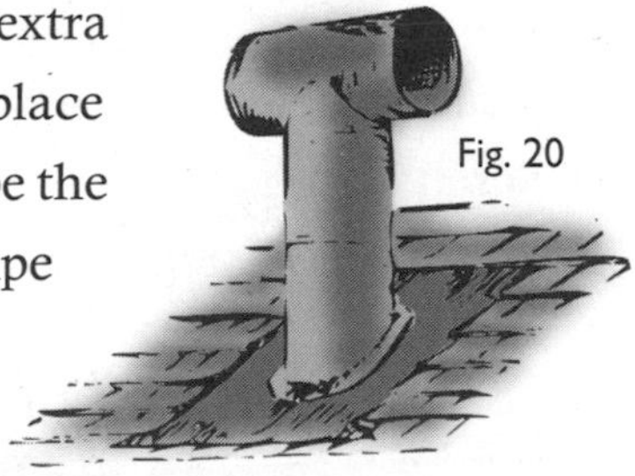

Fig. 20

# 18

# THE FUNNEL
# FIRE-PLACE

This style of fire-place is made by building a foundation about a foot thick of stone and cement enclosed by logs. The top should be paved with brick or cement, for if stones are used so as to come in direct

Fig. 21

contact with the fire, they will burst from the heat, and even if they do no damage you will be reminded of a Fourth of July celebration.

This fire bed should be about four and a half feet square. About a foot and a half above this foundation place a large sheet-iron funnel (Fig. 21), say three feet in diameter at the lower extremity, and taper it up to the smoke pipe, which should be about twelve inches in diameter; fasten the funnel and pipe together and suspend both from the ceiling, the top end of the pipe extending above the roof. This, when constructed, will form a fire-place open on all sides. It will give abundance of heat, and if placed in the middle of the room will warm all parts of it quite evenly.

# 19

# CHIMNEY THIMBLES

A sheet-iron thimble should be built into the chimney flue wherever a smoke pipe is wanted. The thimble should be six and a quarter inches in diameter and four inches long.

# 20

# FIRE CRANE

We are all of us more or less familiar with this useful article. It should be made of a good stiff iron bar braced to an upright piece at right angles. The vertical piece should have pins to fit into sockets, thus making a hinge; the socket part is built into the brick work by the mason while he is building the fire-place. The arm should extend within about six inches of the side of the fire opening, and have dangling hooks on which to hang the kettles (see Fig. 18).

Now that the heavy work of the cabin is completed, you can give your attention to the finishing touches, and whatever may add to your general comfort and the delights of camp life.

# 21

# FRAMES

The door and window frames are usually made of boards one inch thick, planed on one side, with the stops nailed in place hold the sash in position. The window sill should pitch outward and extend over the log underneath, so that the rain will not run to the inside of the cabin.

# 22

# WINDOWS

The windows may be made in a variety of ways, so that the sash will slide sidewise, up and down, or swing in and out. But whichever way you decide to have them, be sure and get them storm-proof. The windows that swing in are the least so of all, and should be avoided for this reason, and because the sash would be in the way when open.

# 23

# SASH

The sash may be procured at the factories, already painted and glazed. One and a half inches thick will answer well enough. The mill people will so crate them up that there is little danger of breaking the glass in the course of transportation.

# 24

# FLY SCREENS

Make a frame just large enough to fill the openings, both for doors and windows. The former should have a latch, and hinges like any ordinary door. Make these frames of one by three inch strips of wood framed or halved together at the corners. Place small, triangular blocks in the angles These will serve the purpose of braces, and keep the frame stiff and from sagging. Over this frame stretch as tightly as possible fine mosquito netting, and securely tack it to the frame. A small batten or strip should be nailed over the outer edge of the cloth and to the frame, to permanently secure the netting.

# 25

# WINDOW HINGES AND FASTENERS

Strong pieces of leather, such as old boot tops, will make good window hinges; but of course, iron hinges are better. Swing windows hinged in this way should have a hardwood bar to hold them open at particular angles (Fig. 22). The bar should be about one inch square, hinged at one end to the sash; the other end should have holes bored through it to fit over iron pins

Fig. 22

placed on the sill of the window. A hook and staple or leather hasp is needed to hold the sash shut. The ordinary sliding sash needs only a button to keep it closed; but if it slides up and down, several will be needed to hold it open at various positions.

# 26

# SHUTTERS

Each window frame should have a loose shutter (Fig. 23), to close the cabin up tight when it is left at the end of the camping season. These shutters should be made the exact size of the log or frame opening. Make them of matched boards with cross-pieces, nailed with wrought nails. Take the corners off the battens or cross-pieces and place them so that they will just fit in the sash opening; put one long bolt through the batten at each

Fig. 23

end of the shutter, extending through the side of the sash and shutter-bars on the inside of the cabin. Place a nut and washer or, better still, a thumb-nut, on the end of the bolts, to draw the shutter tight to the window frame The bars should extend across the opening the shortest way, and be stiff and strong.

# 27

# DOORS

Make your doors (Fig. 24) of matched boards with good wide battens, top, bottom and middle, with braces to keep from sagging.

Nail all together with wrought nails, as they are easily clinched.

Doors might be made of squared sticks framed together (Fig. 25), with braces and cross-pieces of

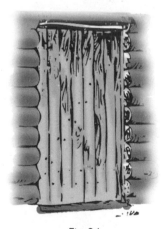

Fig. 24

Fig. 25

thinner material, which should be shingled on the outside. The stick on the hinge side of the door might run up and down and form pivots or shoulders on which the door could swing.

# 28

# DOOR HINGES

A good wrought-iron hinge is the best that you can get, but failing to have any, screw a pivotal stick (Fig. 26) from top to bottom on the edge of the door, so that it will extend into a round hole in the floor, and a corresponding one in the log over the top of the opening.

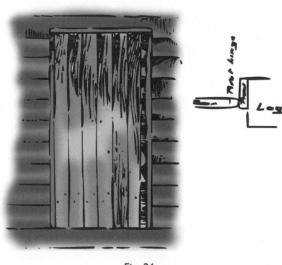

Fig. 26

The bottom end of the pivotal stick must not extend through the floor, or if it does, there must be a log or some kind of bearing underneath to keep it from settling down.

The hole at the top of the opening is to be bored deep so that the pivot or hinge stick may be raised up and slid down into the lower hole. The pivot should be fitted to work easily by shaping and oiling. Then securely fasten it to the edge of the door.

# 29

# DOOR FASTENINGS

The door fastenings may be made of wood, and in principle somewhat like the ordinary iron latch (Fig. 27). The bar should be about two inches wide, one inch thick, and twelve or fifteen inches long. Fasten the pivotal end with a screw or bolt.

The guard should be strong and have a slot long enough to admit of the bar- locking and being raised out of the catch. The catch should be three-quarters of an inch thick, with an incline so that the bar will slide

Fig. 27

into the notch. The guard or guide should be so placed that the bar will just touch on the lower side when resting on the bottom of the slot. The latch is lifted from the outside by a leather or rawhide string fastened to the loose or latch end of the bar and passing through a hole in the door some distance above the latch. Tie a small stick on the outside end of the string, and the latch is complete.

# 30

# CAULKING

To ensure a perfectly storm-proof cabin, the spaces between the logs must be caulked; but defer this as long as you can, so that the logs will get as dry as possible. This work you will be obliged to repeat the second season, and so it is well to leave the general finish of the cabin until the following year, at least if part of the finish should go over the face of the logs. The caulking is done with oakum or moss forced into the joints from both sides of the logs with a wooden, wedge-shaped chisel, struck with a mallet. Cement may be used in place of the oakum or moss.

# 31

# INSIDE WORK

The face of the logs on the inside of the cabin may be made to look quite finished by hewing the faces to a perpendicular plane (Fig. 28), which is done with the broad-axe as the work progresses.

A rough appearance on the inside of the cabin may be had by simply peeling the logs, and a still rougher one by not removing the bark.

Fig. 28

# 32

# WAINSCOT, ETC.

It gives a home-like appearance to cover the logs on the inside of the cabin with matched and beaded boards. The finish is neat and easily kept clean, but it smacks a little too much of the town. It is much better to cover with bark or shingles, and illustrations of both methods are given in the sketches (Figs. 29 and 30). The shingles or bark may be cut in patterns and thus make a good wainscot. If the inside is to be shingled, let the sides of the door or window frames come flush

Fig. 29

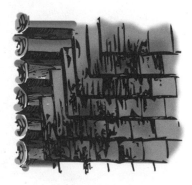
Fig. 30

with the inside face of the logs. The shingles are then to extend nearly to the openings and cover the joint between the frame and the logs (Fig. 31).

Casings may be made of slabs sawed about three inches wide, or by flattening small saplings and nailing them at the side of the openings in the same manner as casings. A wainscot may be made of shingles or bark as above, but laid in patterns to a height of six feet from the floor and capped with a slab or ordinary board to form a shelf (Fig. 32), under which a round stick or a piece of slab may be placed as a molding.

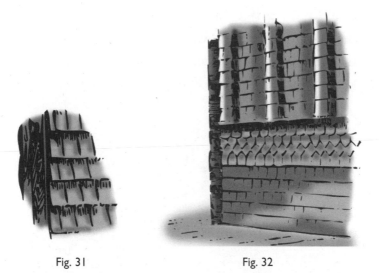

Fig. 31                    Fig. 32

# 33

# STAIRS

Make the supports of strong timbers and frame or cut the steps into them. The newel may be made of a rough stick and the rails of rough poles; the balusters, too, may be rustic. The newel post might be made to run to the ceiling and a screen formed of rustic work (Fig. 33). To do this, fill in the triangular space between the post, the ceiling above and the outside supporting timbers of the staircase with small branches placed like lattice work, or in some other geometrical pattern.

Fig. 33

# 34

# WINDOW SEAT

This may be made by building a frame of good strong sticks, supported by rustic brackets or crooks, the seat being made of small straight sticks, about one inch in diameter, laid close together (Fig. 34).

These seats, to be comfortable, will need to have cushions made of some stout material, such as heavy canvas, and stuffed with twigs of evergreen, white birch bark or shavings. Of course, the appearance may be greatly improved by covering with bear, deer, or other kinds of skins.

Fig. 34

# 35

# BEDSTEADS

Get four good strong posts for the corners, left with the bark on; and to these either frame in or bolt stout cross and side pieces. The posts may run up and form a canopy if you choose. Lay from head to foot of the bed even-shaped springy pieces of wood, a couple .of inches in diameter; put side, foot and head pieces on top of these to keep the boughs in place. These boughs are to serve the purpose of a mattress and the sticks are to act as springs. If you want to use regular springs

Fig. 35

and mattress at any time, you have only to place them on the top of the frame already constructed (Fig. 35). This frame will serve as the foundation of a very simple or an elaborate piece of furniture, and the work added should be so placed as to form braces and stiffen the construction.

# 36

# BUNKS

Place a number of small, even, and straight poles, about two inches in diameter, on two cross beams, one beam at each end of the poles (Fig. 36). These are placed with the head a little higher than the foot. The poles, which are laid close together, are then covered with boughs of evergreen to a depth of eight or ten inches. These boughs should be small and pulled off the limb, not cut with the knife, as the cutting process leaves the sharp ends to stick into you. The bunk should be built at least a foot above the ground to give a free circulation of air.

Fig. 36

# 37

# CHAIRS

Get two high posts for the back, and two legs of the height of a seat for the front. Frame in cross-pieces, as in the bedstead, and make the seat of small, straight sticks, laid close together (Fig 37), or stretch a stout piece of canvas or deer skin across. The usual bracing should then be made and the spaces filled with rustic work.

To make a stool get a log about one foot in diameter and saw from the end of it a block about three inches

Fig. 37

in thickness; bore three holes in this block, each one and one-quarter inches in diameter; then drive pegs or legs into these holes (Fig. 38). A back may be made by nailing upright pieces on the back of the block, extending to the floor and high enough for the shoulders to rest against. These back pieces will then need bracing in the usual way.

Fig. 38

# 38

# WOOD-BOX

Construct a stiff frame of stout round sticks with smaller pieces nailed on the inside to form the sides and bottom, so that the pressure of the wood will not force them off (Fig. 39), or it may be made in regular log-cabin fashion, as shown in Fig. 40.

Fig. 39                         Fig. 40

# 39

# TABLES

To make a rough table, set four corner posts firmly in the ground, nailing cross-pieces on top, or make a frame-work like the bedstead. Cover the top with packing-box boards that you may have brought to the camp, or flooring, or pieces split out of soft wood logs; if of the latter, true them up into slabs. Nail cross-pieces on the table legs at the right height for seats, and let them extend out each side of the top (Fig. 41); on these cross-pieces nail slabs or boards to form the seats.

Fig. 41

Fig. 42

The whirligig table (Fig. 42) is made in the ordinary way with a rustic frame and a smaller table whirling in the centre on a pivot stick, as shown in the sketch. On this whirling part you can place all the general dishes and each individual may be able to help himself.

# PANTRY

Make a dish closet or cupboard by fastening up a packing box, with the cover hinged as a door; a catch to hold it shut may be made with a bit of leather and a nail; also, fasten in some shelves between top and bottom of the box (Fig. 43). This will make a place for keeping knives, forks, dishes, coffee, tea, etc.

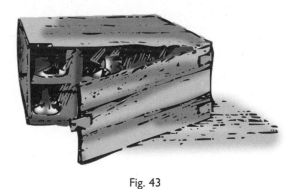

Fig. 43

# 41

# TIN ROOM

In the larger cabins a regular tin-room should be made, say about seven feet square. Ceil this on all sides with matched boards, and then completely line it, floor, ceiling, side walls, and door, with tin. This will be a storage place for bedding, blankets, etc., or anything that the wood mice, squirrels or hedgehogs will gnaw, while you are away from camp.

# TONGS

Take a good tough piece of green wood one and a half inches in diameter and three feet long, ash, hickory, elm, or wood that will bend easily, and cut the stick half away for the distance of a foot in the centre (Fig. 44).

Then heat this part over hot coals until it will bend together without splitting. Now whittle them nicely into shape and put a cross-piece in, and pin the two arms together as shown in Fig. 44. The ends of the tongs should be so shaped that they will catch hold readily of anything that has dropped into the fire, such as a piece of bacon or pork. The poker is simply a round stick, three or four feet long, with a notch cut in one end so that a pail or kettle may be lifted from the fire.

Fig. 44

# 43

# TO HANG PAILS OR KETTLES OVER THE FIRE

Drive two stout crotched sticks, one each side of the fire, and an additional one on which to swing the cross-stick when taking a pail or kettle off the fire. The cross-stick should be a good stiff piece, about two inches in diameter.

# 44

# BROOMS

Make them by laying hemlock twigs around a small stick and binding them firmly with stout cord foot long, cut from a piece of white birch, tied on in a similar way, will also make a very good broom; indeed, the best of all kinds, if well made.

Then cut off the ends and trim evenly (Fig. 45). Splinters, about one foot long, cut from a piece of white birch, tied on in a similar way, will also make a very good broom; indeed, the best of all kinds, if well made.

Fig. 45

# 45

# REFUSE OF CAMP

Dig a good-sized hole in the ground in which to throw refuse meat, fish, potato parings, dishwater, etc. Every time anything is put in it sprinkle on a little of the earth that was taken out. It will keep away a good many bad odors and not make an attraction for the flies.

# 46

# TO KEEP BUTTER HARD

If your camp is by a cool stream or spring, you can put your butter, etc., in the water. A very satisfactory cool place may, however, be made by sinking a barrel in the ground and covering the top with mosquito netting and the whole with a few hemlock boughs.

# ICE HOUSE

An ice house is a luxury in the woods, but where the encampment is permanent it will be of great use in keeping meats and game. You can have it filled with ice in the winter by your guide. An ordinary small log building is just the thing, built half underground and with room enough above ground to get in through a door in the gable end. After the logs are laid up and the roof is in place, spike vertical pieces on the inside and sheath with matched boards. Then fill the space between sheathing and logs with moss well rammed into place. Begin putting the boards on at the bottom and put in the moss as the work progresses. Two doors, one on the inside and one on the outside, will answer ordinary purposes, but a hollow door, packed with moss, will give the best protection. Pack the ice in moss, or, better still, with sawdust, if it can be procured.

# 48

# SPRING

If you can find a wet piece of ground near your cabin, dig out a large, deep hole, providing you find that it will fill with cold water, or, if you have a running brook, make a spout out of the bark of a small tree and so arrange that a pail maybe placed under the lowest end to catch the running water.

# TEMPORARY SHELTERS

# THE INDIAN CAMP

This primitive form of shelter (Fig. 46) may be made by partially cutting the trunk of an evergreen tree about five feet from the roots, just enough so that it will fall to the ground, leaving the butt end fastened to the stump. Cut off the boughs from the underside so as to

Fig. 46

make a comfortable space beneath. Take these boughs, and some cut from other trees, and place them over the small tree, which serves as a ridge-pole but with the small end on the ground. Thus you will have a camp similar to the sketch.

# 50

# THE BRUSH CAMP

This camp (Fig. 47) may be made by placing a ridge-pole between two trees which stand about eight feet apart, then putting on a thick covering of large hemlock boughs, placing the top ends down, and making the sides conform to the shape of a tent. The shelter may be improved by thickening up with smaller

Fig. 47

twigs placed in the same manner as the larger ones. Such a shelter with the back closed similarly to the sides and a good camp fire in front may be made very comfortable.

# 51

# THE INDIAN WIGWAM

This shelter (Fig. 48), quickly and easily as it may be made, is one of the best. Its steep sides will stand a

Fig. 48

heavy rain without wetting through, and if well made the camp will be warm and comfortable.

Begin by standing three poles in the shape of a pyramid and lashing them together at the top. Then add other similar poles standing at the same angle, about one foot apart at the butt end, and fastened together at the top. Omit a couple of poles where the entrance comes. Then thatch the outside with evergreen boughs, as in the brush camp. This shelter may be greatly improved by tying horizontal poles in the manner of hoops to which the thatching should be secured.

# 52

# THE BRUSH CAMP IMPROVED

Place two strong crotched sticks in the ground about eight feet apart and some six feet high, with a stout ridge-pole in the crotch. Now place stiff, straight poles from the ridge-pole to the ground making a V shaped frame (Fig. 49). These poles need to be about

Fig. 49

eight inches apart. Thatch on them with boughs of hemlock or cedar laid with the face or feather ends down, beginning at the bottom and working up to the ridge. If these boughs are laid about ten inches in thickness and weighted down with poles on top to keep them from blowing away, you will have a very nearly water-tight shelter.

This kind of a shelter may be improved again by laying the poles or rafters about fifteen inches apart, and tying on smaller poles horizontally about seven inches apart, and making a regular thatched roof, using the hemlock and cedar boughs in place of straw.

# 53

# BRUSH HOUSE

Drive two rows of stakes in the ground about one foot apart for the sides and back of the shelter; the stakes should be about five feet high; fill in between them with boughs (Fig. 50); press and stamp them down and trim off all pieces projecting on either side. Let the corner stakes have crotches at the top to support eave poles; over these poles place rafters about eight inches apart with butt end lying on the ground. Tie them together at the top and pin them down at the butt. Over the rafters tie horizontal strips about seven inches apart. Then thatch as in the preceding case.

Fig. 50

# 54

# THE OPEN "LEAN-TO"

Place two crotched sticks for the front, about seven feet high; lay a pole across these: (Fig. 51) Against this cross bar lean three strong poles, and secure them at the lower end by pushing them well jnto the earth, or by pinning them down with crotched sticks hooking over the poles and driven into the ground. Over these poles lay cross sticks to support the bark or brush covering

If the cover is of brush, then make the angle of the roof quite steep, and as soon as the boughs are in place weight them down with other heavy poles to keep the wind from blowing them away.

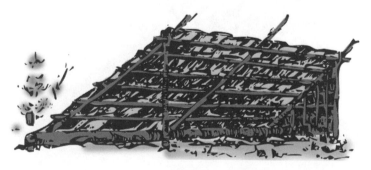

Fig. 51

# 55

# THE BARK CAMP

This is the most common camp that is constructed (Fig. 52). Usually large pieces of bark are taken to form the sides and roof, as is shown in the illustration. If the roof is steep the cross poles or rafters may be laid close together and the cover made of shingles. The top sides of the rafter should be flattened to make good nailing places.

The more extensive cabins are shown in the following illustrations, and the cuts speak for themselves, aided as they are by their titles and the preceding general description of log houses.

Fig. 52

There is shown in the second full-page illustration one of the most comfortable and serviceable of semi-open camps. If possible, it is built with the fire end against a large bowlder; but if one cannot be found of sufficient size, then the front end of the camp may be lined with stone laid up in the same manner as an ordinary wall. This rock or wall fire-place should be of sufficient width and height, so that when a large open fire is built the blaze will not be able to reach the logs and burn them.

The camp may vary in dimensions from eight feet wide and twelve feet long up to almost any size; but one twelve feet wide and sixteen feet long would probably be the best both for convenience, comfort and economy. The logs are laid up as in an ordinary log cabin to a height five feet above the ground on both the sides and ends. This will give sufficient space at the back or eaves end of the camp. The sides and front end are then raised to the height of the door, and the top logs extended over the opening on the sides and the bowlder in the front end of the camp to bind the structure together. The logs coming under the top ones are fitted to each side of the rock which forms the fire-place. The roof should extend from the back end of the camp to a point about four feet in front of the bunk. This will make a covered space of sufficient size so that the cooking may go on and the table be set during stormy weather. The rafters should be six inches in diameter and be placed horizontally, resting on the sides of the camp. They should be placed about two feet apart, and the one in front of the camp should be eight feet from the ground, so that a man will have sufficient head-room in the space in front of the bunk. The logs forming the sides and ends of the camp should have the spaces between them chinked with moss or closed by nailing small saplings in the angles.

The cover or roof is made of two thicknesses of bark, well lapped and extended over the sides and back, so that water cannot drip into the camp.

To prevent these camps from smoking during windy or heavy weather, the following precautions should be taken: First, cut only such trees as lie close to the camp. This will make a space through the top of the trees for the smoke to rise in, and the other trees round about will act as wind guards. Second, raise the sides and end round the fire nearly as high as the peak of the roof. Third, make the smoke opening or space not covered by the roof rather small. In this way you will form a chimney-like draft for the smoke. An additional wind-guard may be placed over the fire, as shown in the first full-page illustration, in the semi-open camp.

The fire-bed should be raised to the height of the bunk, not only to assist the draft but so that the heat will be readily reflected into the camp. To do this a large log or a row of stones are placed in front of the fire, and the space from that point back to the bowlder is filled in with earth or gravel

The usual pole for hanging pails over the fire may be improved upon by placing a small log across the fire end of the camp. To this pole suspend long wires, reaching nearly down to the fire, with hooks on the ends.

The bunk may be constructed as described on page 36, figure 36, or the bearing poles may be made of logs split into slabs and laid in the same manner as a floor. On top of this the boughs or sprigs need to be placed to at least a depth of ten inches. When the door is hung, the roof made tight, and the bunk comfortable, this will be found one of the most desirable camps that can be constructed.

Plan

*Plan*

102

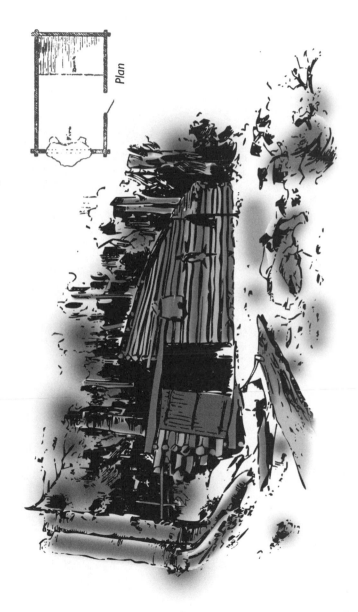

Plan

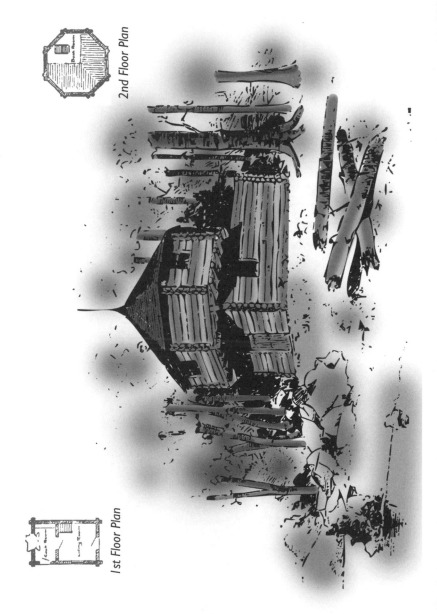

2nd Floor Plan

1st Floor Plan

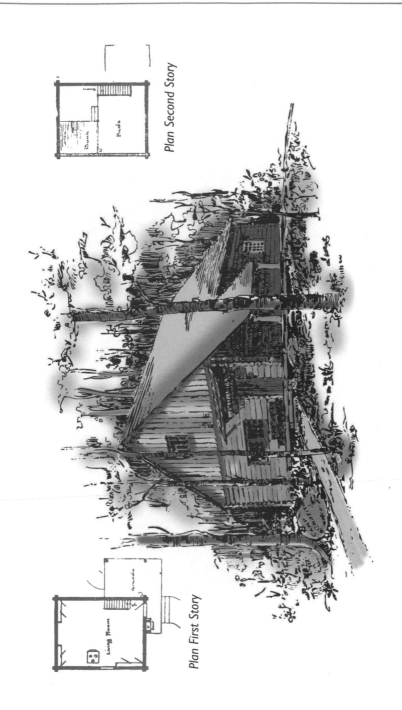

Plan Second Story

Plan First Story

Floor Plan

*Dog Kennels*

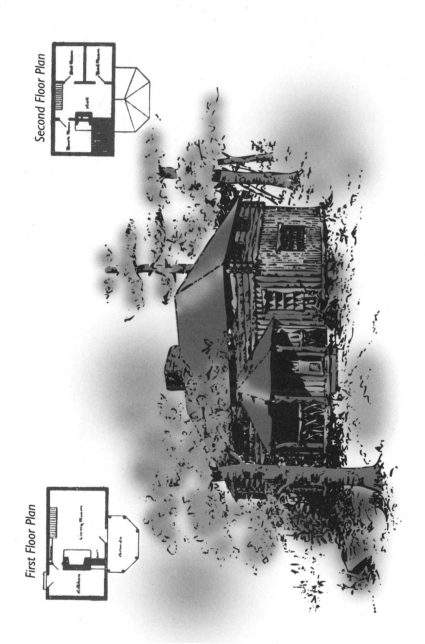

Second Floor Plan

Bed Room
Bed Room
Closet
Bath Room

First Floor Plan

Living Room
Kitchen
Porch

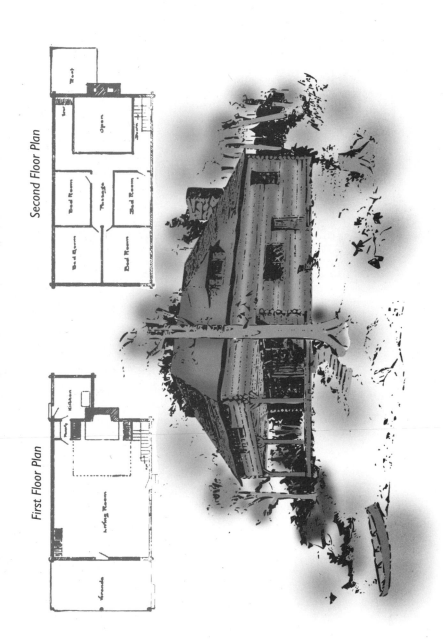

Second Floor Plan

First Floor Plan

109

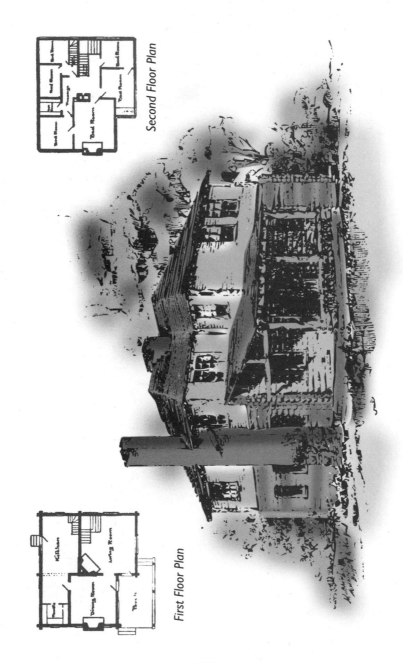

Second Floor Plan

First Floor Plan

110

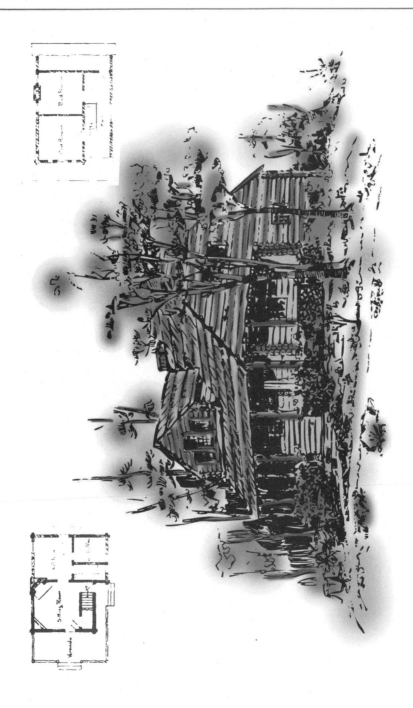

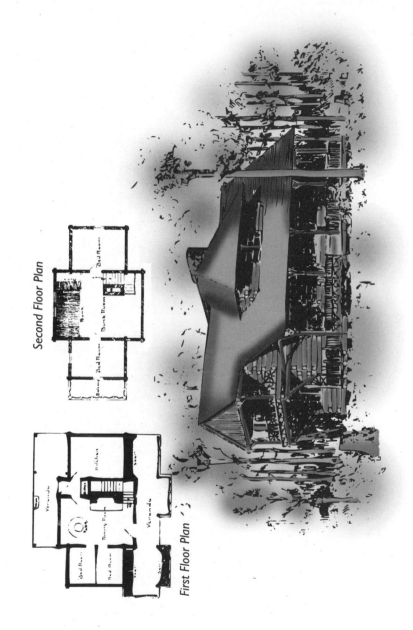

Second Floor Plan

First Floor Plan

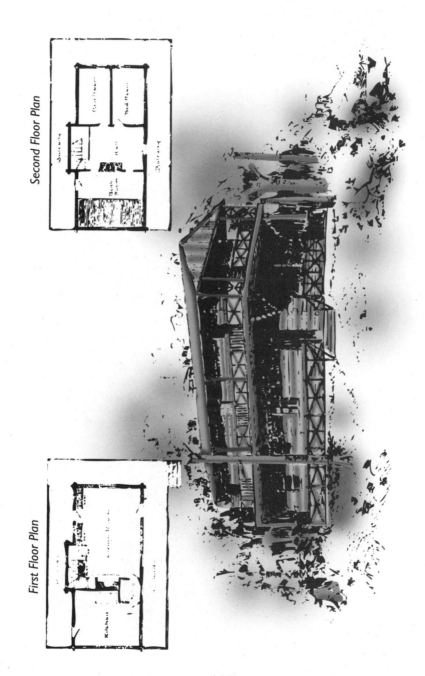

Second Floor Plan

First Floor Plan

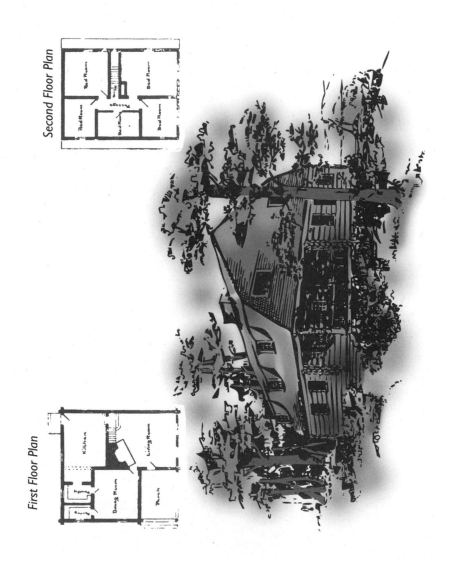

Second Floor Plan

First Floor Plan

Second Floor Plan

First Floor Plan

*Second Floor*

*First Floor*

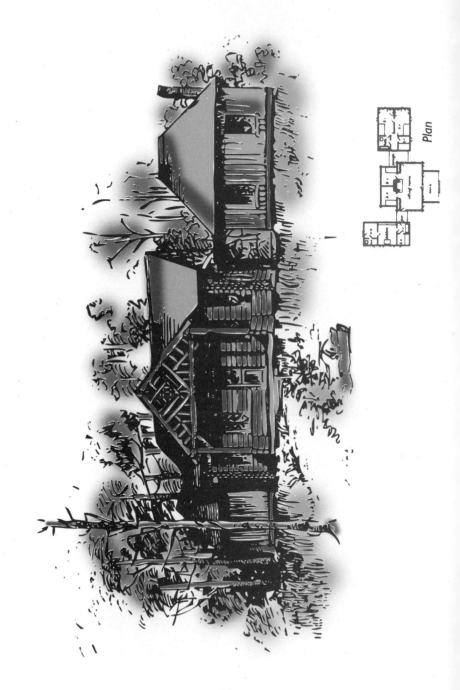

*Plan*

122

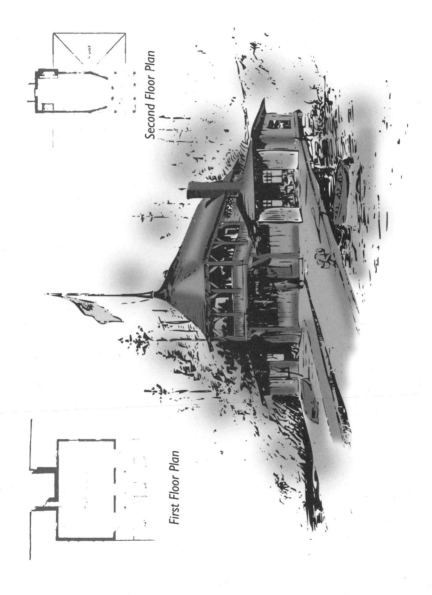

Second Floor Plan

First Floor Plan

*Plan*

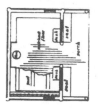

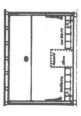

Plan

Scat
Scat
Scat

Seat

Seat

# RESOURCES

## BOOKS

*Building A Log Cabin Retreat: A Do-It-Yourself Guide*, by Michael Mulligan. Paladin Press, 2002

*Build Your Own Low-Cost Log Home*, by Roger Hard. Storey Publishing, 1985

*The Classic Hewn-Log House: A Step-by-Step Guide to Building and Restoring*, by Charles McRaven. Storey Publishing, LLC, 2005

*How to Build and Furnish a Log Cabin: The Easy, Natural Way Using Only Hand Tools and the Woods Around You*, by W. Ben Hunt. Collier Books, 1974

*"How-to" Build This Log Cabin for $3,000*, by John McPherson. McPherson, 1999

*How to Build Your Dream Cabin in the Woods: The Ultimate Guide to Building and Maintaining a Backcountry Getaway*, by J. Wayne Fears. Skyhorse Publishing, 2010

*How to Build Your Own Log Home and Cabin From Scratch*, by S. Blackwell Duncan. Tab Books, 1978

*How to Build Your Own Log Home for Less Than $15,000*, by Robert L. Williams. Loompanics Unlimited, 1996

*Little Book of Log Cabins: How to Build and Furnish Them*, by William S. Wicks. Dover Publications, 2005

*Living Homes: Stone Masonry, Log, and Strawbale Construction*, by Thomas J. Elpel. HOPS Press, LLC, 2010

*Log Cabins and Cottages: How to Build and Furnish Them*, by William S. Wicks. Nabu Press, 2010

*Log Cabins: and How to Build Them,* by William Swanson. The Lyons Press, 2001

*Log Construction Manual: The Ultimate Guide to Building Handcrafted Log Homes,* by Robert Wood Chambers. Deep Steam Press, 2006

*Rustic Retreats: A Build-It-Yourself Guide,* by David Stiles. Storey Publishing, 1998

# WEB SITES

## 20-20 Site

This site offers a step-by-step guide to building log
cabins and has links to free information, brochures,
estimates, and resources.

www.2020site.org/cabin/index.html

## Learn to Build A Log Home

Author Robert W. Chamber's site with free log
building information, dates for workshops, and
links to his book, DVDs, tools he recommends,
and other Web sites.

www.logbuilding.org

## The Outlands

A short course in log building. Includes
comprehensive illustrations.

http://outlands.tripod.com/farm/logcabin.htm

## Log Home Builders Association

The Log Home Builders Association is a non-profit
educational organization whose mission is to help
men and women around the world build their
own log homes from scratch, and in many cases
build without a mortage. Offers helpful articles

from subjects like kit log homes to termites and everything in between. Also gives information about their famous two-day log home classes. www.loghomebuilders.org

**Alaska Antler Works**

One couple shares their step-by-step tips on how to build a log cabin (in Alaska, specifically) from preparing the land to giving the home log spiral stairs. The site is very detailed with pictures and accompanying tips for every step. www.alaskaantlerworks.com/Alaska_cabin.htm

**Our Log House**

A site run by a couple building their own log cabin. It is a journal that follows the planning and building of their cabin in Darrington, Washington. www.ourloghouse.com

**Mother Earth News**

Bill Sullivan boasts a step-by-step plan to build a log cabin for $100. Includes pictures of the cabin he and his wife built. www.motherearthnews.com/Green -Homes/1981-05-01/Log-Cabin.aspx

**Wholesale Log Homes**

Sells high quality milled heartwood logs, timbers,
    finished boards, log siding, and log cabin home
    accessories. Does not sell log cabin plans or model
    log home kits.

www.wholesaleloghomes.com

**Log Home Neighborhood**

An online log home community for log home
    enthusiasts.

www.loghomeu.com

**International Log Builders' Association**

A worldwide organization dedicated to furthering
    the craft of handcrafted log building to the
    advancement of log builders, and to the promotion
    of the highest standards of their trade.

www.logassociation.org/index.php

**Great Lakes School of Log Building**

Offers courses for people with an avocational interest
    in log building. No construction or carpentry
    background is needed, nor is any unusual strength
    required—just a strong motivation to learn log
    building and a willingness to abide by school rules.

www.schooloflogbuilding.com/index.htm

**Lasko School of Log Building**

Teaches handcrafted log construction in several styles
for application in both residential and commercial
projects with time-honored traditional skills.
Also teaches log home care and maintenance and
restoration practices.

www.laskoschooloflogbuilding.com

**Log Home Today**

Offers information regarding log homes and kits for
sale, decorating ideas and furnishings, log home
building supplies and tools, and allows you to
follow Eric, Laura, and Veronica and their do-it-
yourself projects.

www.loghometoday.com

# NOTES AND PLANS

Use these pages to make notes and
sketch your cabin plans.

_____
_____
_____
_____
_____
_____
_____
_____
_____
_____
_____
_____
_____
_____
_____
_____
_____
_____
_____

# LOG CABINS

# LOG CABINS

# LOG CABINS

WILLIAM S. WICKS

# LOG CABINS

_____
_____
_____
_____
_____
_____
_____
_____
_____
_____
_____
_____
_____
_____
_____
_____
_____
_____
_____
_____
_____
_____
_____
_____
_____
_____
_____
_____
_____
_____
_____